It's easy to have a
CATERPILLAR
visit you

Advisory Editor

Caroline O'Hagan

Illustrations by

Judith Allan

LOTHROP, LEE & SHEPARD BOOKS
NEW YORK

A caterpillar is a little creature that will in time turn itself into a moth or butterfly. The adult moth or butterfly lays eggs, which hatch into caterpillars that eventually turn themselves into moths or butterflies.

If you have a caterpillar visit you, you can watch how it does it.

You can find caterpillars in fields, woods, parks and gardens. Look especially under leaves.

When you find one, pick it up very gently or try sliding it onto a piece of paper.

Never try to catch a caterpillar that has a **hairy** body. These can be **poisonous** and **dangerous.**

When you catch your caterpillar, make sure you take plenty of the leaves you found it on, because these are what it eats. Most caterpillars are very fussy and will eat only their favorite leaves.

You can use a box or a big glass jar for your caterpillar's new home. Make sure the lid has holes in it, so your caterpillar can breathe. It will need lots of its favorite leaves to eat. Every morning sprinkle a little water on it and its leaves, to replace the morning dew it would get outdoors.

Try to count how many legs your caterpillar has. Most caterpillars have three pairs in front and four to six pairs behind. All along the sides of its body are breathing holes — nine pairs of them. And how many eyes does it have? You should be able to count twelve!

If you listen hard while your caterpillar is eating, you may hear it munching and crunching. Its little jaws are very strong and, unlike you, it chews sideways!

As your caterpillar eats it gets fatter and fatter — too fat for its skin. And so, from time to time, it sheds a skin. It makes a fine thread, attaches it to a leaf to keep itself steady, then struggles out of its old skin and crawls away with a lovely new one.

After it has shed its skin several times your caterpillar will be ready to start turning into a moth or butterfly. It spins a cocoon — lots and lots of fine thread — round its body to make a safe home while it changes. While it is inside its cocoon it is called a chrysalis.

If your caterpillar turns into a chrysalis, you must look after it very carefully. Keep its jar in a cool place, away from direct sunlight. **Never** bang it, shake it, or move it. It may stay a chrysalis all through the winter. If it does, just sprinkle it with a few drops of water from time to time. The chrysalis does not need to be fed. It is using the food that was stored in its body while it was a caterpillar.

If you want to put your caterpillar back before it becomes a chrysalis, **remember** to put it back on the same leaves it was eating when you found it.

But if you keep the chrysalis, you may be lucky enough to be watching when the moth or butterfly crawls out from one end. At first the moth or butterfly will be damp, but quite quickly it will stretch out its wings to dry. Take the jar to the place where you found your caterpillar and remove the lid. Let the moth or butterfly climb out by itself. If you try to help, you might damage it. When it is ready, it will fly away to find a mate. The female will then lay eggs on its favorite leafy plant and they will eventually hatch into caterpillars.

Text copyright © 1980 by Culford Books Limited
Illustrations copyright © 1980 by Judith Allan

All rights reserved. No part of this book may be reproduced or utilized in any form or by any means, electronic or mechanical, including photocopying, recording or by any information storage and retrieval system, without permission in writing from the Publisher. Inquiries should be addressed to Lothrop, Lee & Shepard Books, a division of William Morrow & Company, Inc., 105 Madison Avenue, New York, New York 10016.
First published in the United States of America in 1980.
1 2 3 4 5 6 7 8 9 10

Edited, designed, and produced by Culford Books Limited, 135 Culford Road, London N1, England.
Edited by John Goldsmith.
Designed by Judith Allan.

Printed by Waterlow (Dunstable) Limited, England.

Library of Congress Cataloging in Publication Data

Main entry under title:

It's easy to have a caterpillar visit you.

SUMMARY: Gives instruction for catching a caterpillar, housing and feeding it, and what to do when it turns into a chrysalis.
1. Caterpillars—Juvenile literature. 2. Caterpillars as pets—Juvenile literature. [1. Caterpillars as pets] I. O'Hagan, Caroline. II. Allan, Judith, (date)
QL544.2.I87 595.7'8'0439 79-3456
ISBN 0-688-41947-X
ISBN 0-688-51947-4 lib. bdg.